THE WILD WORLD OF ANIMALS

THE WILD WORLD OF ANIMALS
GIRAFFES
JILL KALZ

CREATIVE EDUCATION

Published by Creative Education, 123 South Broad Street, Mankato, Minnesota 56001. Creative Education is an imprint of The Creative Company. Designed by Rita Marshall. Production design by The Design Lab. Photographs by Corbis (Theo Allofs, Karl Ammann, Bettmann, Tom Brakefield, Pierre Colombel, John Conrad, Jerry Cooke, Tim Davis, Nigel J. Dennis; Gallo Images, Gallo Images, Peter Johnson, Wolfgang Kaehler, Larry Lee Photography, William Manning, Joe McDonald, Richard T. Nowitz, Paul A. Souders, Wendy Stone, Larry Williams). Copyright © 2006 Creative Education. International copyright reserved in all countries. No part of this book may be reproduced in any form without written permission from the publisher. Printed in the United States of America. Library of Congress Cataloging-in-Publication Data: Kalz, Jill. Giraffes / by Jill Kalz. p. cm. — (The wild world of animals). Includes bibliographical references and index. ISBN 1-58341-350-2. 1. Giraffe—Juvenile literature. I. Title. II. Series. QL737.U56K35 2005. 599.638—dc22. 2004062593. First edition 9 8 7 6 5 4 3 2 1

Everything about it is an exaggeration. Its long neck. Its gangly legs. Its large, dark eyes. Even the length of time it spends in its mother's womb: 15 months, one of the longest **gestation** periods in the animal world. Just an hour after its birth, the baby giraffe stands on wobbly knees and looks out at the African landscape. It is a dangerous place for a newborn, filled with lions, hyenas, and leopards. Hiding places are rare. But for this baby, the grassy land is home. And within 24 hours, the young giraffe will be running across it.

Giraffes' long necks make them easy to recognize

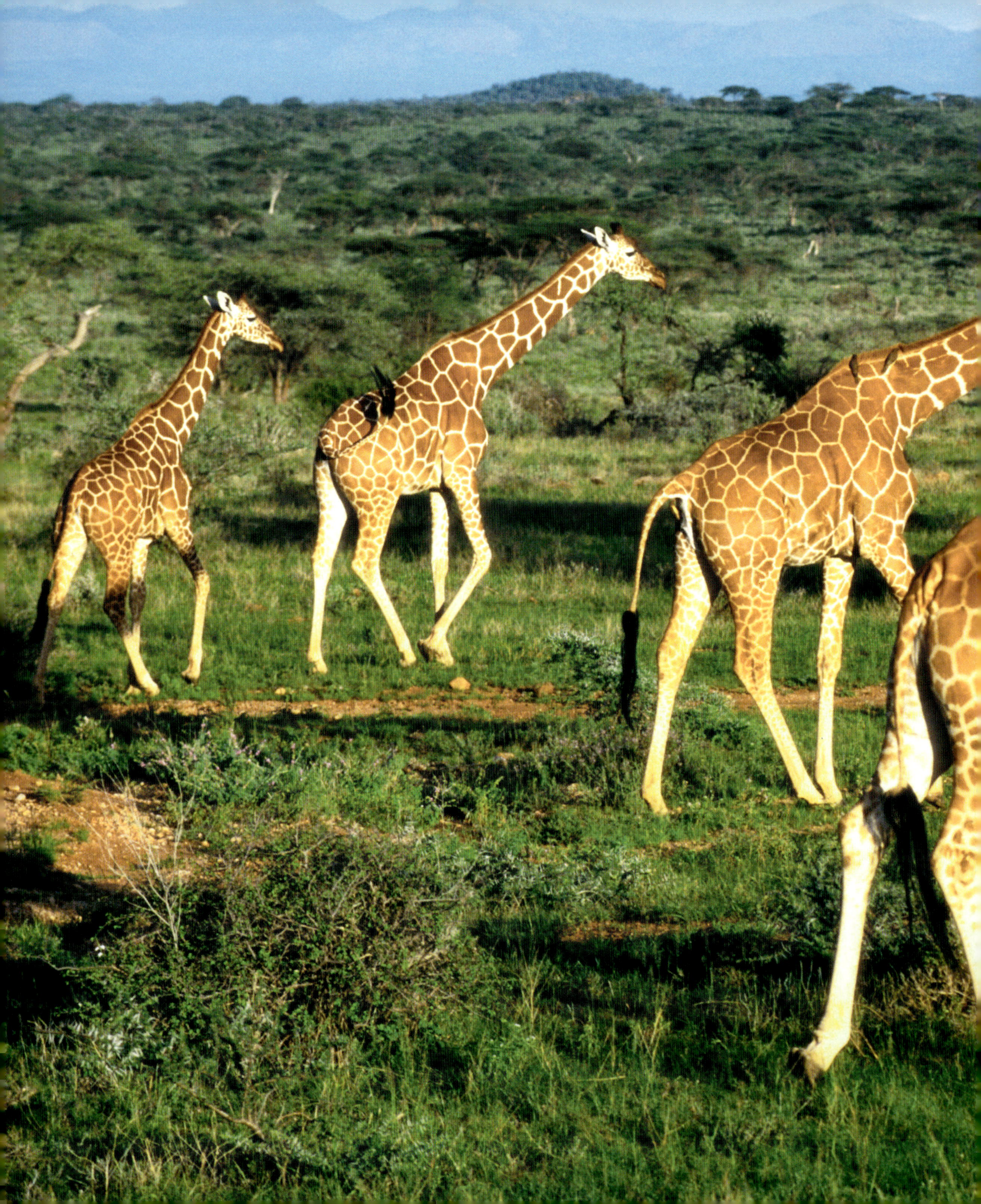

LOOKOUT TOWERS

Giraffes are the tallest animals on land. Males stand between 15 and 18 feet (4.6–5.5 m) tall and weigh up to 3,000 pounds (1,360 kg). Females are usually smaller, but not by much.

Almost half of a giraffe's height is its neck

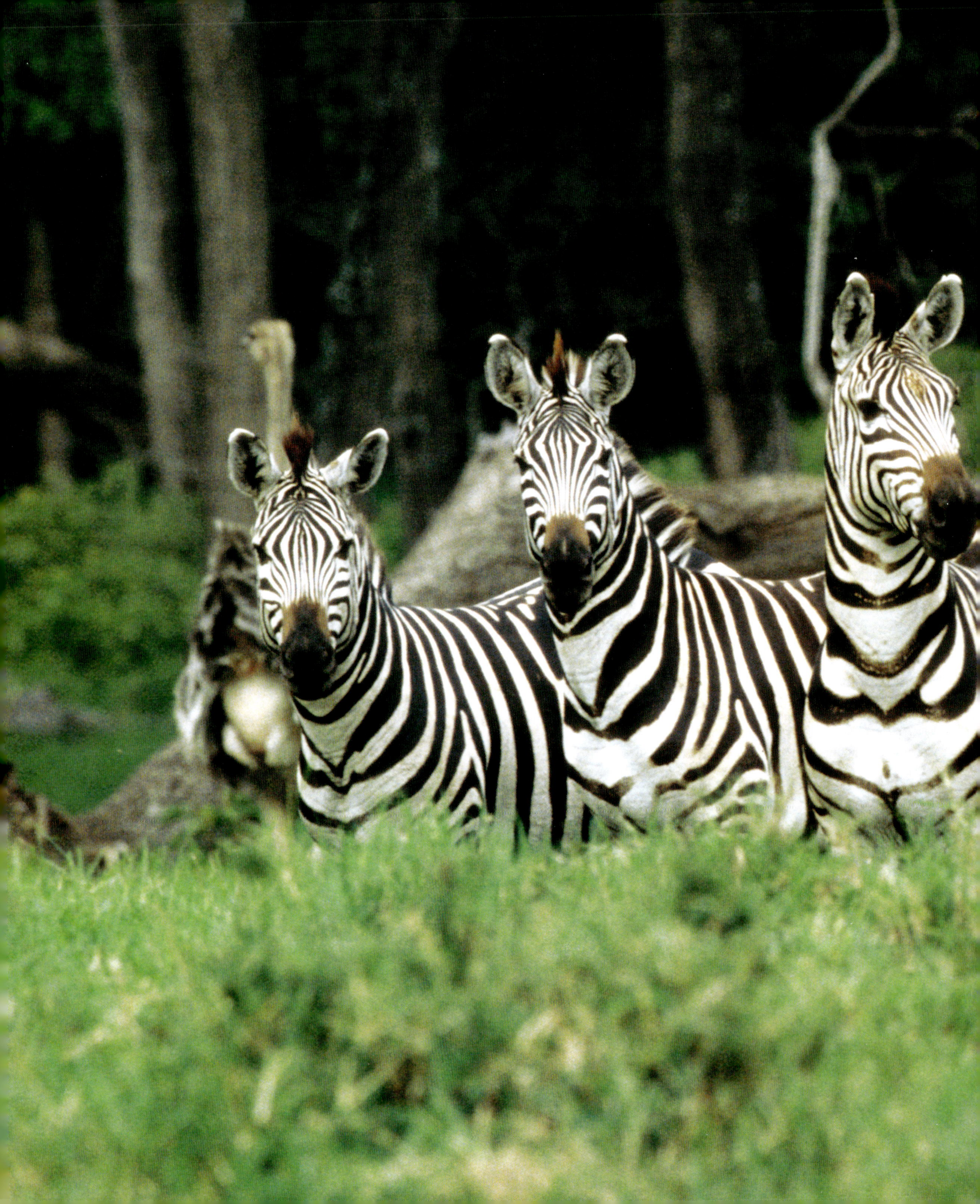

There are nine different types of giraffes. They live in the open forests and tree-dotted **savannas** of eastern and southern Africa. Their height and excellent eyesight make them natural "lookout towers." Antelope, zebras, ostriches, and other animals often rely on giraffes to warn them of approaching **predators**.

Giraffes share their home with zebras and ostriches

No two giraffes look exactly alike. The pattern of brownish blotches on a giraffe's short, dense fur is as **unique** as a human fingerprint. But general patterns appear regularly and can be used to identify the region in which a giraffe lives. The reticulated giraffe, for example, has large brown patches separated by very thin white lines. It can be found only in East Africa. The patterns and colors on a giraffe's skin help **camouflage** it against the trees.

Even though they're called "horns," the bumps on a giraffe's head are not true horns. They are just bony growths covered by a thin layer of skin and topped with black hair. Both male and female giraffes have these bumps.

Some giraffes have round or leaf-shaped spots

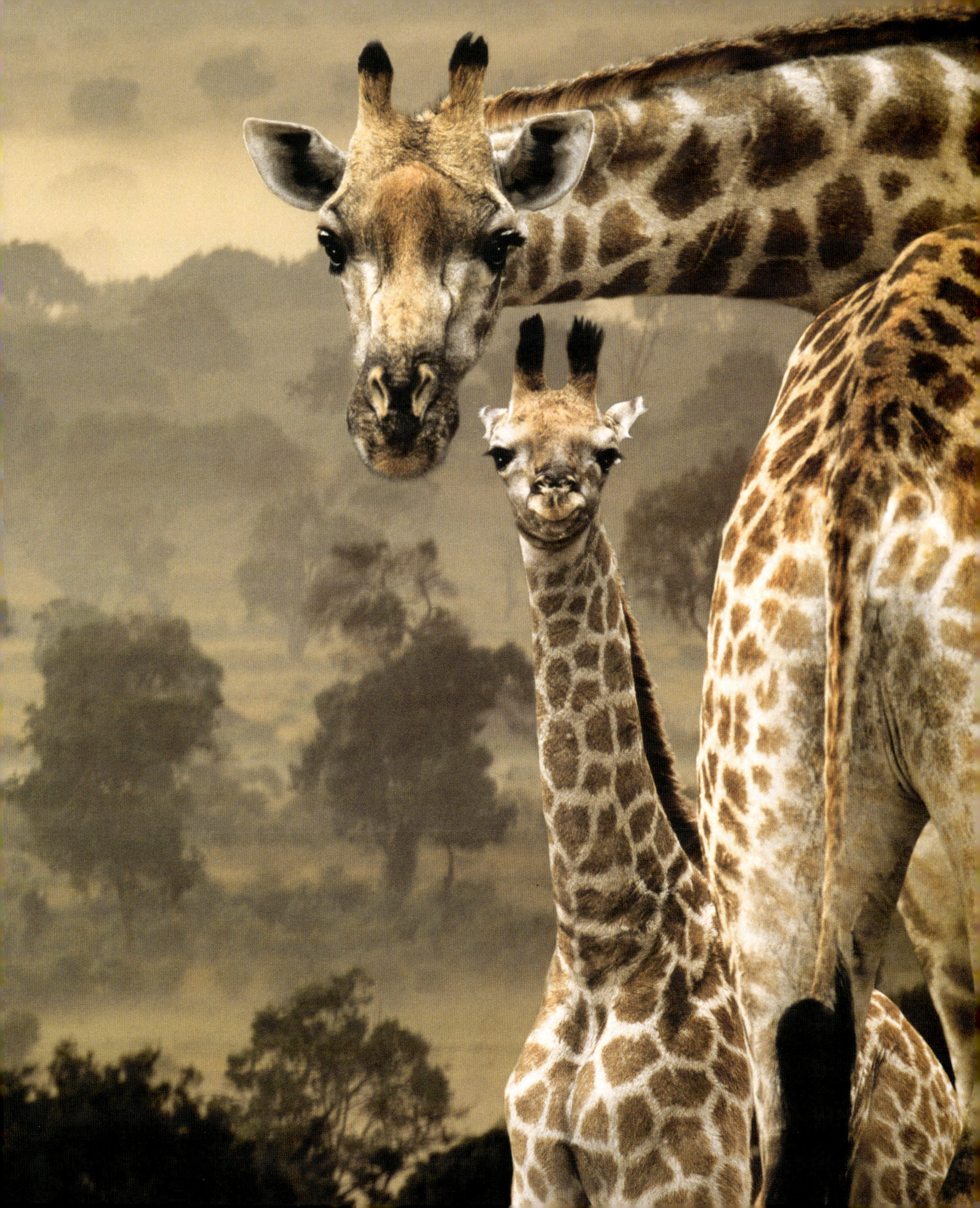

The giraffe's most outstanding feature is its neck. Just seven **vertebrae** support it. Humans have seven vertebrae, too, but the giraffe's neck bones are much larger. Inside the giraffe's long neck, a special system of blood vessels controls the flow of blood to and from the head. Without this system, a giraffe would faint every time it raised or lowered its head. The rush of blood would damage the animal's brain.

Giraffes have the longest neck of any animal in the world

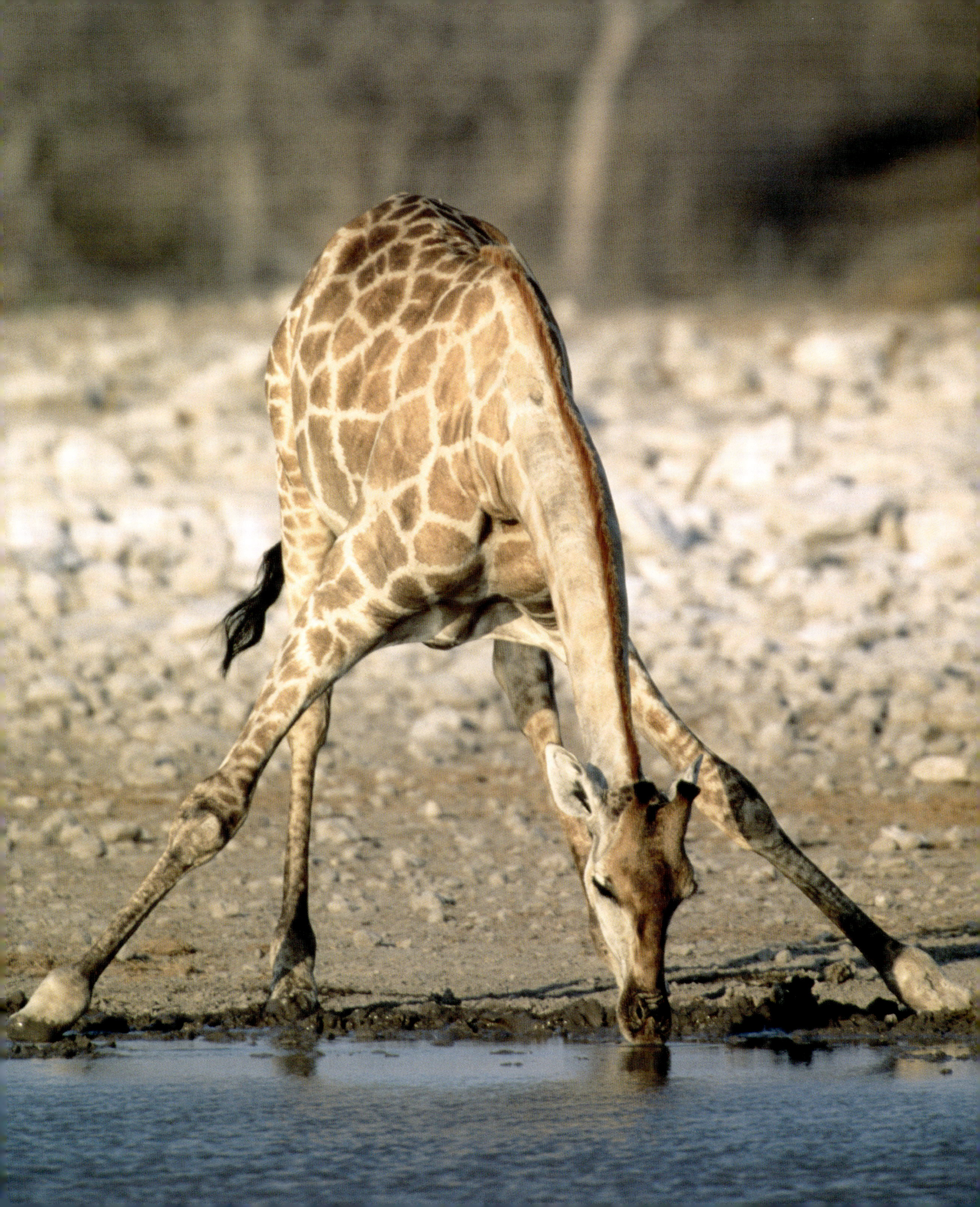

Giraffes have huge feet—larger than dinner plates! Their walk is slow and graceful but rather unusual. They move both legs on one side forward at the same time; first their left legs, then their right. If they didn't walk this way, their long legs would tangle with every step. Giraffes cover a lot of ground

The African plains provide plenty of space to roam

when they walk, too. Each step covers about 15 feet (4.6 m). When threatened, giraffes run much like rabbits. They move both front feet together, then swing both hind legs forward, planting them in front of their forefeet. At a full run, giraffes can reach a speed of 35 miles (55 km) per hour.

Giraffes' powerful legs can also serve as weapons

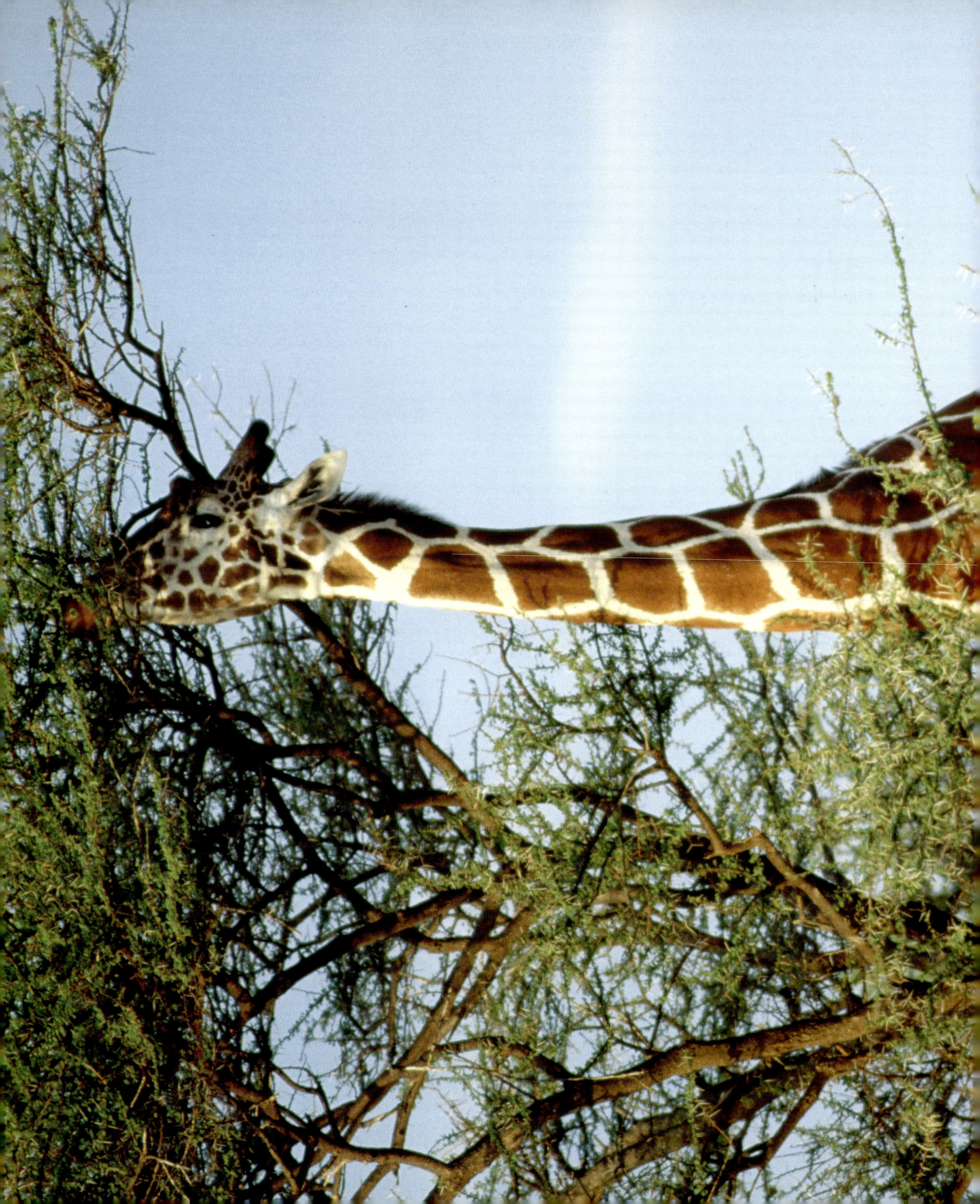

LIFE AS A GIRAFFE

Giraffes sleep very little, and when they do, it's just for a few minutes at a time. They spend most of the day eating. Giraffes are browsers, which means they eat leaves from trees or bushes. They grab the leaves with their long, tough upper lip and their muscular tongue, which can be more than 18 inches (45 cm) long. Acacia tree leaves are a giraffe favorite.

Giraffes eat up to 75 pounds (34 kg) of food a day

Giraffes eat quickly and usually swallow their food before it's been properly chewed. Some time later, they bring small amounts of the partially digested food back up their throats and into their mouths. Then they chew it more completely and swallow it again. This is called "chewing cud," or ruminating.

Even though its neck is incredibly long, a giraffe can't quite reach the ground without widely spreading its front legs.

18 Giraffes are vulnerable to predators when drinking

This makes getting a drink difficult. Luckily, giraffes can go days or even weeks without taking a drink, getting all the water they need from the green plants they eat.

Giraffes live in herds of about 10 members. They are gentle, quiet animals and communicate with one another mainly through body language. But they do make some noises. Giraffes may bleat, whistle, grunt, snort, or moo like a cow.

A young giraffe may bleat to get its mother's attention

Male giraffes occasionally challenge one another to "duels." These contests help males establish rank, or position, in a herd. During a duel, two males twist their necks around each other, trying to determine their opponent's strength. This activity is called "necking."

Giraffes mate year-round. Female giraffes are very affectionate, protective mothers. They give birth standing up, the baby dropping to the ground below. Despite the great distance it falls, the baby, called a calf, is

Mothers with calves often stay close together

rarely hurt and is usually standing on its own and nursing on its mother's milk within an hour.

At birth, a baby giraffe stands about six feet (1.8 m) tall, but despite its size and its mother's protection, the first year of a calf's life is extremely dangerous. Leopards, wild dogs, and hyenas are all threats. More than half of all calves don't survive their first year. If he or she is one of the lucky ones, however, a giraffe may live up to 25 years in the wild.

Female giraffes take turns "baby-sitting" for calves

GIRAFFES AND PEOPLE

Thousands of years ago, giraffes roamed all across Africa. Herds of 100 members were not uncommon. Ancient African cultures spun stories about the giraffe's origins, believed it had spiritual powers, and hunted it to fulfill a variety of basic needs. They used its meat for food and its **hide** to cover shields.

Ancient peoples painted giraffes on cave walls

The ancient Egyptians mistakenly believed that the giraffe was a cross between a camel and a leopard. They called it a "camel-leopard," a name that has followed the giraffe to the present day in its scientific name: *Giraffa camelopardalis*.

Giraffes have a small, camel-like hump on their back

Until a few hundred years ago, giraffes were rare outside of Africa. Because of this, giraffes were sometimes sent as diplomatic gifts (gifts from one government to another), much like panda cubs from China today. One of the earliest records of such a gift dates to 1415, when a giraffe was sent from Kenya to China.

Non-Africans quickly fell in love with the giraffe. In 1827, people in Paris, France, got their first look at a live giraffe, and its visit nearly caused a riot. Soon, Parisian women were fixing their hair in "giraffe" style, piling it on top of their heads and sometimes tucking in a hair comb with a picture of a giraffe on it. Men started wearing spotted coats that looked like giraffe skin.

24   People once sported giraffe-inspired fashions

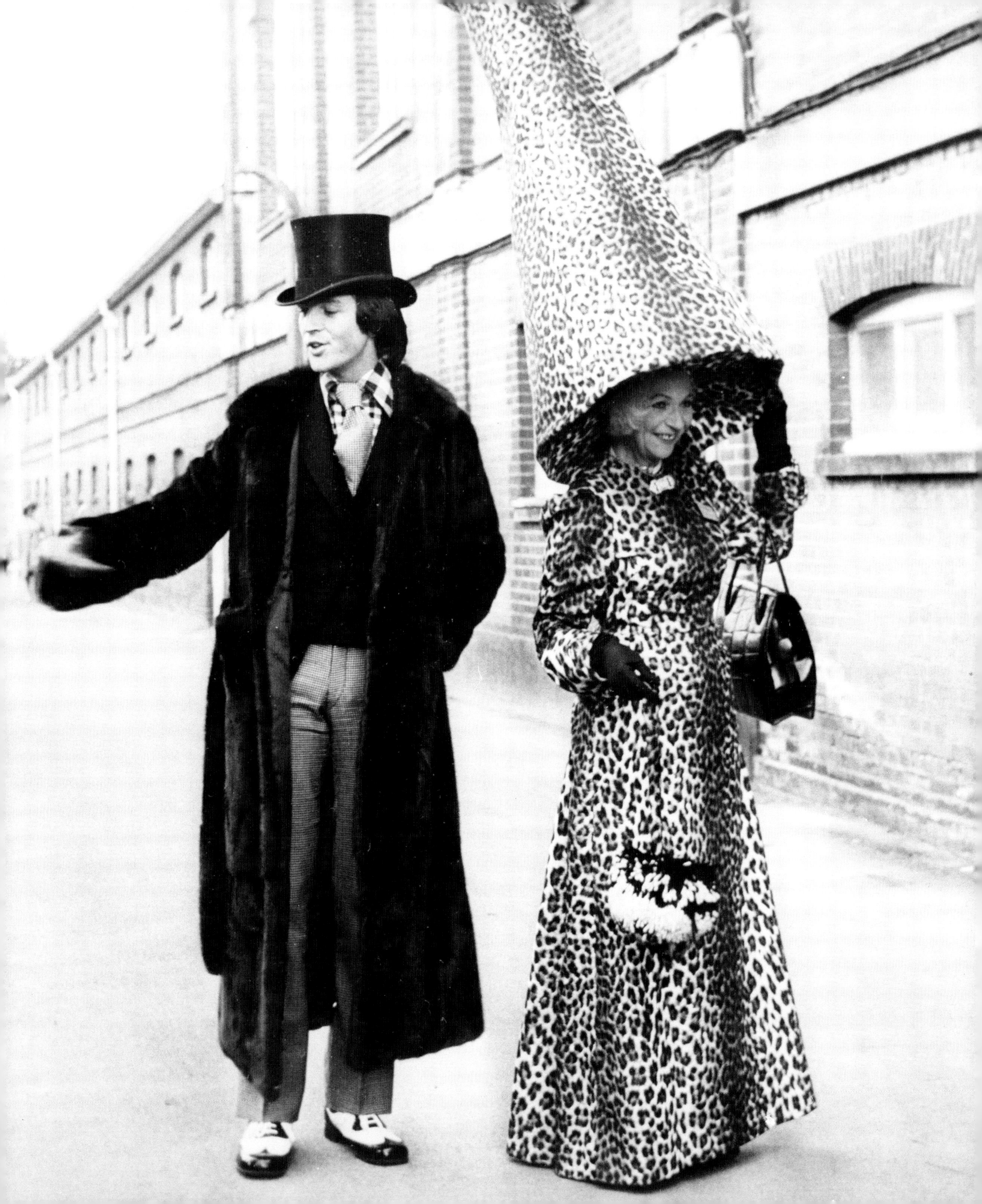

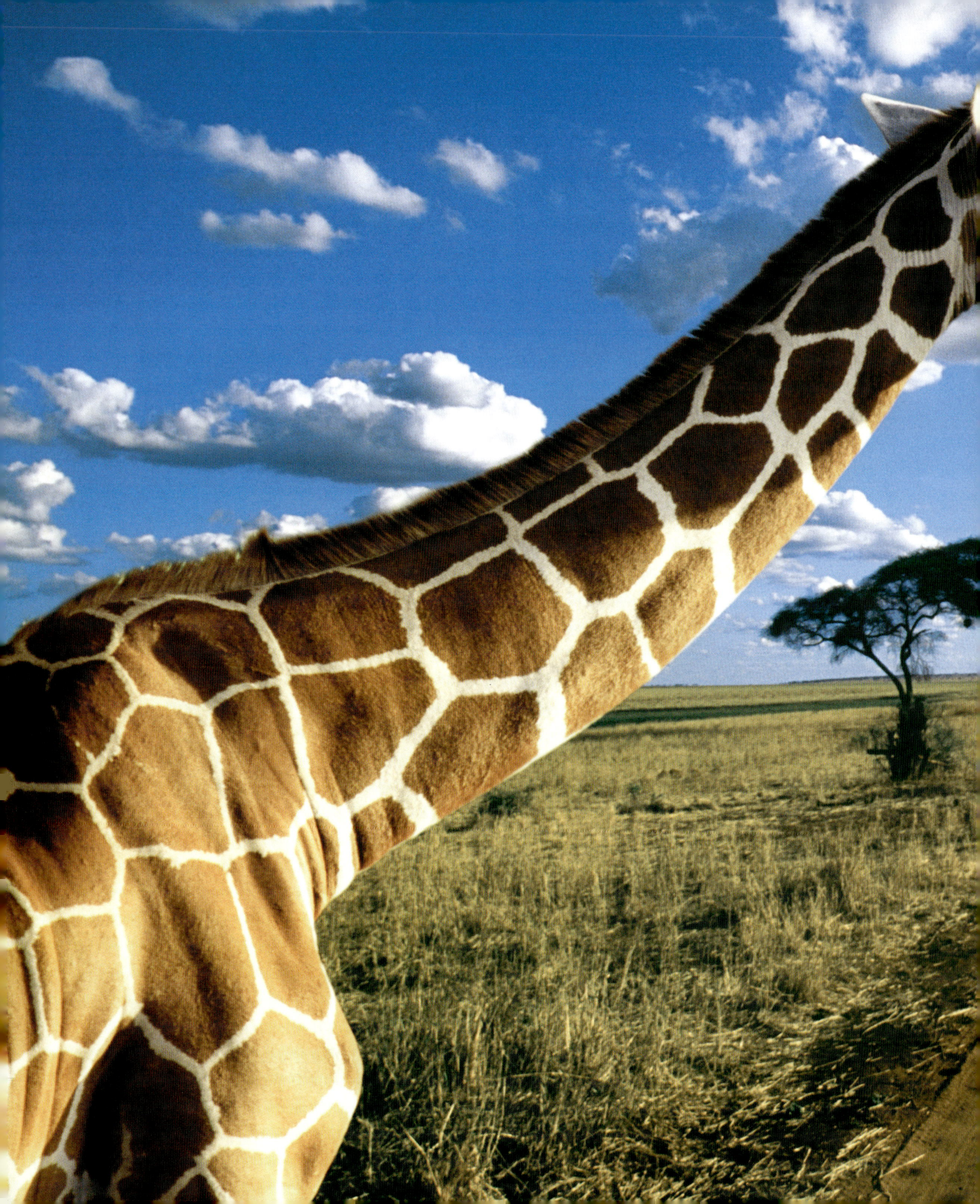

Today, some people in Africa still hunt giraffes for their tough yet nutritious meat and their hides, hair, and tails. Giraffe tails are prized for use in good-luck bracelets and thread for sewing or stringing beads. They're also used as fly swatters. Some countries have now made hunting giraffes illegal, but **poachers** continue to take their toll.

Dirt roads cross through giraffes' homeland

As human populations in Africa continue to grow, more and more of the giraffe's natural **habitat** is being lost. People need land on which to build their homes, grow crops, and raise animals. As a result, trees are cut down, and giraffes soon find themselves with no food and no home. Although the giraffe's survival is not in immediate danger, **conservationists** are keeping a close eye on the situation.

Trees are crucial to giraffes' survival

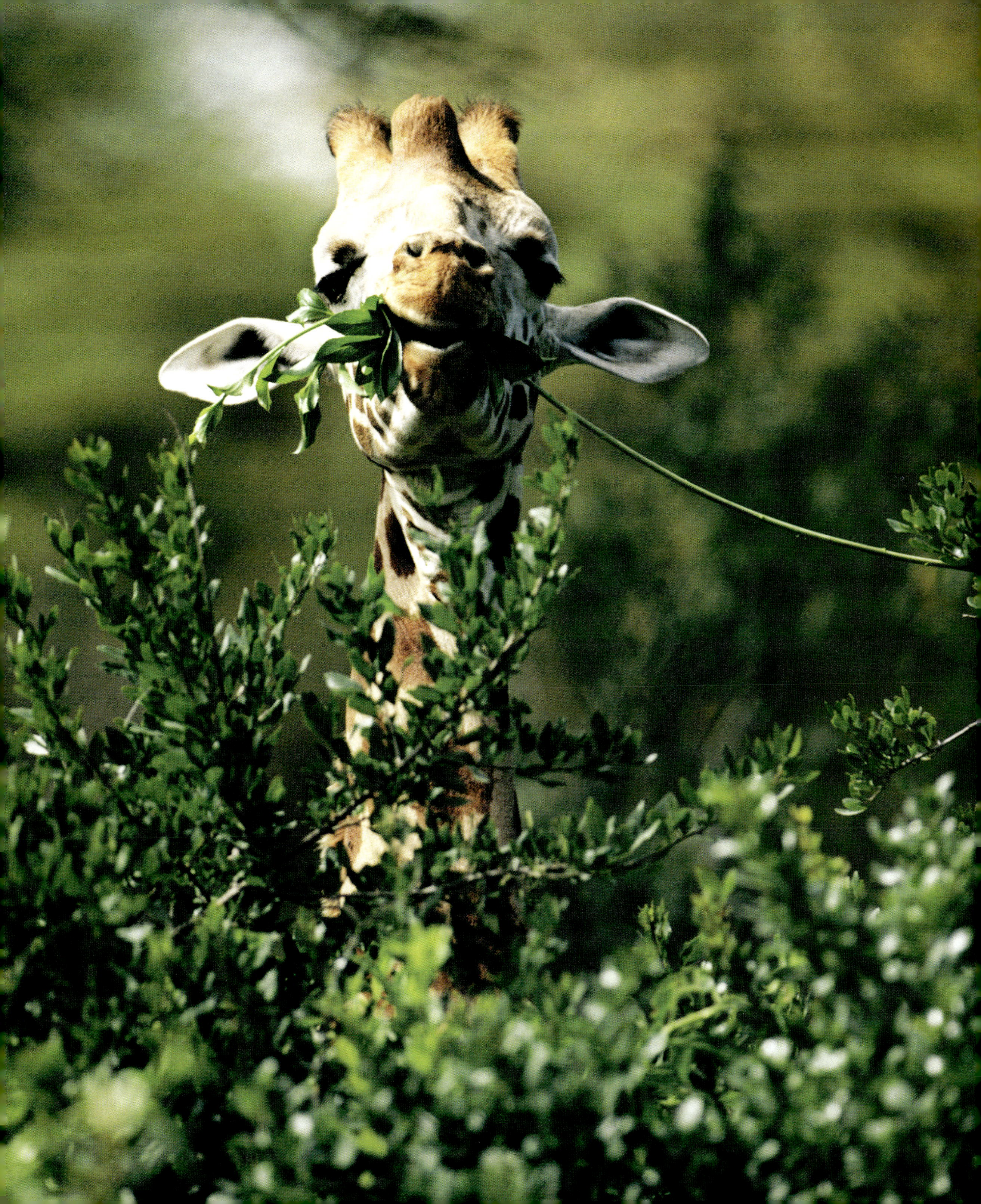

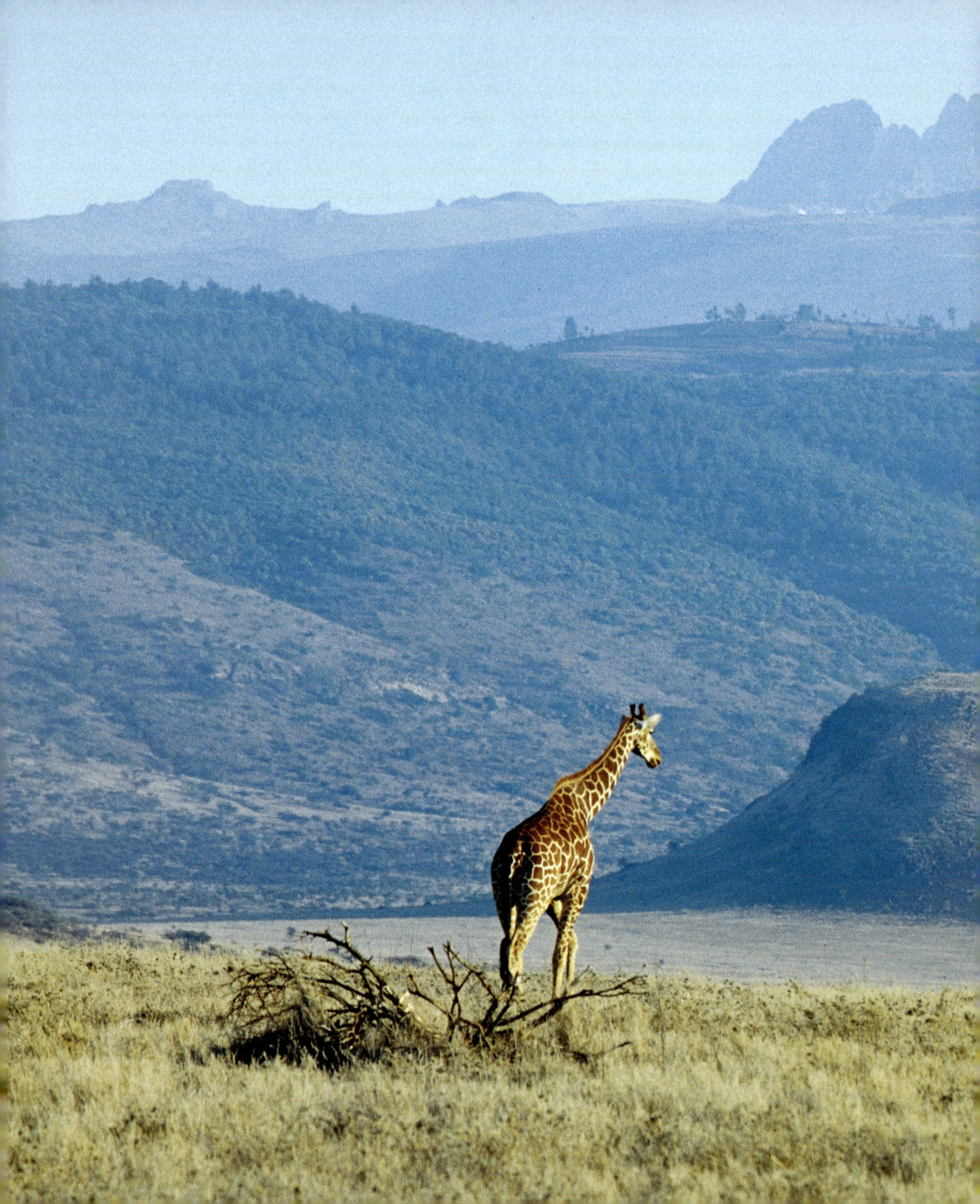

Even though the world has changed tremendously since people saw their first giraffe thousands of years ago, we continue to share a sense of wonder with them. Our ancestors treasured the giraffe for its exaggerations and its quiet nature, and whether we see it on TV, in a zoo, or in the wild, we'll continue to treasure this curious-looking creature for all the same reasons.

Today, giraffes still tower above the African grasslands

GLOSSARY

Camouflage is coloring that helps make an animal hard to see in its surroundings.

People who work to preserve Earth's natural resources are called **conservationists**.

An animal's **gestation** period is the amount of time it takes an unborn baby to develop in its mother's womb.

The place where a creature lives is called its **habitat**.

A **hide** is the skin of an animal, often used to make clothing.

Poachers are people who hunt animals illegally.

Predators are animals that kill and eat other animals.

Savannas are flat grasslands in hot areas of the world.

Something that is **unique** is one of a kind.

The bones that make up an animal's backbone, or spine, are called **vertebrae**.

BOOKS

Markert, Jenny. *Giraffes*. Minneapolis: The Child's World, 2001.

Parker, Barbara Keevil. *Giraffes*. Minneapolis: Lerner Publishing Group, 2004.

Wexo, John B. *Giraffes*. Poway, Calif.: Wildlife Education, 2001.

WEB SITES

Creature Feature: Giraffes http://www.nationalgeographic.com/kids/creature_feature/0111/giraffes2.html

Giraffes http://www.giraffes-giraffes.com

Giraffe: Smithsonian National Zoological Park http://nationalzoo.si.edu/Animals/AfricanSavanna/fact-giraffe.cfm

INDEX

Africa 5, 9, 10, 22, 24, 27, 28	habitat 5, 9, 28, 32	necking 20
calves 5, 20–21	herds 19, 22	size 7, 21
communication 19	humans 12, 22–23, 24, 27, 28, 31	threats 5, 21, 27, 28
Egyptians 23	life span 21	travel 14–15
food 17–18, 19	mating 20	types 9, 10
fur 10	neck 5, 12, 18, 20	water 19